A Cup of

Mint Tea

Kindness to Family, Supplication, and
Other Short Stories to Warm the Heart

Volume 2

BY IMAN ABDALLAH AL-QAISI

Illustrator
Nadia Yousef

Translators
Maha Mustafa
Rama Malak
Jeanan Kanaan

Copy Editors
Lena Abedrabbo
Aisha Zeben
Dima Almeniawi

Layout and Graphics

pandaUXstudio.com
Thought. Action. Interaction.

Acknowledgements

Besides those who are mentioned here, my deepest gratitude and prayers extend to all of those who have worked tirelessly on this publication, shared it with others, or remembered it in supplication. This work simply could not have been completed without you; All praise be to God.

My special heartfelt thanks goes to: Fatma Almaery, Sumaiya Gavell, Afraa Jasim, Freda Shamma, Yamama Al-Alusi, Ahmad Teleb Mostafa, Fedaa Jasim, Hanan Abu Salah, Jackie Othman, Abdullah Khatib, Lamis Ahmed, Hadia Mahmoud, Arsalan Ahmed and Allison Carpenter.

"Oh, My Lord, Increase Me in Knowledge!"

Many beneficial books were written before mine, and I have long admired them and profited from them spiritually. Numerous collections have always inspired me in my teachings and lectures. Every time I have prepared an instructional topic, I have established the habit of praying for the scholars who have enlightened me through their invaluable publications. I am fortunate to have been able to spread beneficial teachings learned from my study of their works, yet it never occurred to me that I, too, might one day be an author, sharing my own books with others. All praise is due to God as He has made this experience a pleasant and joyful task.

Twenty-seven years ago in the United States, I began to work in Islamic schools. I started by teaching Arabic and Quran, and I began to use stories from Islamic history in order to engage my students in the lessons. I later moved on to teach Islamic Studies in schools, throughout Muslim communities, as well as in programs for mainstream Americans interested in learning more about Islam. It was an arduous task to locate stories that would address the diverse topics I wanted to explain. Therefore, I dedicated many hours to research in order to collect the best stories for my work, ones that brought to light the morality, values, and devotion espoused by the Islamic faith.

Two years ago, I initiated a model for the teaching of the Quran, the first program of its kind in the United States. I wove together teachings of the Quran, *Tajweed* (Elocution, the proper pronunciation of Quranic recitation), as well as Islamic stories. The stories I selected illustrated proper manners and behavior, as well as experiences during the life of Prophet Muhammad (PBUH)[1] and the *Sahaba*, his companions. This new method allowed for a more in-depth teaching of the Quran, as I carefully cited references for my sources as I taught. The students found the lessons enjoyable and easy to absorb.

In my books, I strive to make the readings understandable for children, teachers, parents, and readers of all ages. Educators may themselves use these writings as a tool to instruct others. Additionally, the stories span a vast time frame, from the time of the earliest prophets to the modern day. I have deliberately selected stories that are concise in order to keep them engaging, fresh, and never boring. My intention was to make this book simple, yet to have it teach messages that are deeply profound.

May God allow these publications to be useful references for His community (*ummah*). All praise be to God, this book is my second, following a very favorable response to my first work, *A Cup Of Mint Tea: Short Stories to Warm the Heart, Volume 1*. May God give me strength, as my plan is to publish a total of twelve books in this series.

Finally, these books are not the endeavor of just one person, but a joint effort among teachers, friends, family members, and all those who assisted in translating, illustrating, and editing. May this work be counted from among our good deeds and be a witness for us on the Day of Judgment. If what we have written is correct, it is only from the Mercy of God. If there are inaccuracies, they are surely from our own weaknesses.

Iman Abdullah Al-Qaisi

---

[1] Acronym for "Peace be upon him." Common Islamic etiquette dictates prayers of peace to be made for Prophet Muhammad (PBUH) at every written or spoken mention of his beloved name. Etiquette likewise encourages such prayers upon every prophet of God.

CONTENTS

"God does not look at your appearances or your wealth, but He looks at your hearts and your deeds."

Prophet Muhammad (PBUH)
Narrated by Muslim

— 1 —
The Act of Sincerity
The Soldier Who Dug the Tunnel [2]

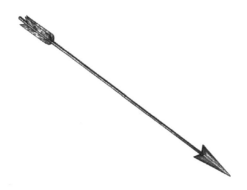

By the first century after the death of the beloved Prophet Muhammad (PBUH), the Islamic Empire had expanded considerably, and the Muslim population had grown dramatically. The leaders of this early community were exceptionally dedicated to their faith. Nevertheless, they did not compel the communities that they encountered to convert to Islam. On the contrary, the Muslims protected Christians and Jews so they could practice their own faiths safely. This tolerance led many to convert to Islam as people were exposed to the faith that was simple and inspiring.

It was during the Umayyad period that the borders of

---

[2] Dalil Al-Sa'ileen, pg. 91, by Anas Ismail Abu Dawud.

the Islamic Empire continued to spread from the Atlantic Ocean in the West to the Indus River in the East.

In one of the battles that the Muslims waged against the Romans, the Muslims, under the command of Maslamah ibn Abd al-Malik, surrounded a city with large, impervious walls. The siege went on for many months. Maslamah ibn Abd al-Malik urged his soldiers to be examples of heroism, resilience, and self-sacrifice in order to penetrate the city. Inspired by the words of his commander, a soldier ran from the midst of the Muslim army and sprinted towards the fortress, his face covered with a scarf.

The enemies launched many arrows at him, trying to prevent him from coming close to the walls of the fortress. However, he held firm and kept running. Death appeared not to worry him. The masked man succeeded in reaching the wall and started digging a tunnel under the fortress. He squeezed himself through the tunnel, got inside, and opened the gates for the Muslim army to enter. In a sweeping assault, the Muslims were victorious.

Maslamah, overwhelmed with happiness, sent out the word that the soldier who dug the tunnel should come forward. No one answered, so he said, "I have ordered my personal guard to let him in, and I swear that it is mandatory that he comes to see me." Maslamah wanted to reward the soldier immensely for his courage.

After a while, a man approached the security guard and asked to see the commander-in-chief. The guard asked, "Are you the soldier who dug the tunnel?"

The man replied, "I have news regarding that solider."

The guard allowed the man to appear before Maslamah.

When he stepped in, he said, "The soldier who dug the tunnel has put upon you three conditions, before he allows you to know his identity. Do you agree to that?"

"Of course," Maslamah replied.

"The first is that you do not identify him to the Caliph. The second is that you do not ask him who he is. And the third is that you shall not try to compensate him for what he has done. Do you agree to these conditions?" the man asked.

"It is agreed," Maslamah said.

The man said in a very humble voice, "I am the soldier who dug the tunnel." No sooner did he finish his words than had he dashed away, running very quickly.

From that day forward, in every prayer, Maslamah prayed to God, "Oh God, grant me companionship on the Day of Resurrection with the soldier of the tunnel."

Lessons Learned:

1. **Encouragement and Motivation Are Keys to Success**
   The commander knew that he alone could not open the fort, so he encouraged his soldiers to do so, urging them to struggle for the sake of God and to consider how they could become part of the solution to this problem. Victory was due to the grace of God first, but also to the simple soldier who was inspired by the encouraging words of his commander-in-chief.

2. **Sincerity in Actions**
   Many people think they are working for the sake of God, but they boast excessively about their accomplishments to the point that their deeds are reduced to nothing more than self-conceit. This results in the reward being reduced to no more than scattered dust from which neither we nor anyone else can benefit. Therefore, always be scrupulous in performing all actions with sincerity. Keep good deeds private in order to attain God's true pleasure and reward.

3. **Wisdom and Sincerity Bring Victory**
   Always be proactive and take initiative. Never assume that any matter that affects the community (*ummah*) is something that cannot be remedied or is beyond one's personal capacity. Rather, consider every matter to be an essential, personal matter and begin to seek its solution. Bear the responsibility of giving victory to the greater community (*ummah*). With this intention, God will help the believers and bless their time and efforts.

4. **Thank People in Order to Thank God**

As a way to thank the soldier, Maslamah was willing to reward him with money, fame, and reputation. Such positive reinforcement is very effective in many situations to encourage people to work harder for the sake of God. Never criticize people for their actions or put them down. Poor treatment not only discourages others, but also prevents them from committing future good deeds.

5. **Actions Are Based on Intentions**

Reward for any action depends on the intention behind it. This soldier risked his life for the sake of God alone. He taught us that no money is equal to the joy of Paradise. Fame and reputation in front of people cannot compare to recognition in front of God and His angels. Wealth in this world will surely end, and only God's glory remains in the afterlife. People too often strive for the temporary rewards of wealth and praise in this life, rather than waiting for the ultimate reward in the hereafter. The Prophet (PBUH) said, "*Verily actions are by intentions, and for every person his reward is judged by what he intended ...*"[3]

6. **Lessons Can Be Taught By Anyone, Regardless of Rank, Age, or Profession**

A simple soldier gave his commander-in-chief a lesson. The sincerity of this soldier had many benefits. One was victory to the Muslims. Additionally, he taught his commander-in-chief, his fellow soldiers, and the Muslim community (*ummah*) a valuable lesson in sincerity. Furthermore, his commander prayed for him from that day forward. What a great reward that he continued to reap!

---

[3] Narrated by Bukhari and Muslim.

"I stayed up all night massaging my mother's feet, and my uncle stayed up all night praying. I think my deed that night was more joyous than his."

Muhammad Ibn Al-Munkadir

— 2 —
How Can I Be Good to My Mother?
My Mother Lied to Me Eight Times [4]

The story starts from the day I was born. I was the only child of a very poor family that rarely had enough food. When we happened to have some rice to eat, my mother used to give me her share. As she put the rice on my plate she would say, "Son, eat my rice; I'm not hungry," and this was her first lie.

After I grew up a little, my mother used to finish the housework and go fishing in a small river next to our house. She hoped to catch a fish for me to eat so that it might help me grow. One time, by God's will, she was able to catch two fish. Excited, she rushed to the house, cooked the fish, and put both of them in front of me. I started eating the fish, savoring

---

[4] Min Rawai' Mustafa Al-'Aqqad, by Mustafa Al-'Aqqad.

the rare feast. She would take the remnants I discarded to eat the remaining meat around the thorny bones. It pained my heart, so I put the second one in front of her to eat. However, she immediately returned it to me and said, "Don't you know that I do not like fish?" This was her second lie.

As I got a little older, the time soon came for me to start school. However, we did not have enough money for school expenses. So my mother went to the market and made an agreement with the manager of a clothing store. Her job would be to go house-to-house, selling clothes to ladies in the neighborhood. One rainy winter night, my mother stayed out late working while I was waiting for her at home. I decided to go out to look for her. I found her carrying the bulky merchandise and knocking on doors, so I called out to her and said, "Let's go home, it is late and really cold; you can always finish this tomorrow." She smiled at me and said, "My son, I am not tired." This was her third lie.

One day I had final exams and my mother insisted on accompanying me. I went inside as she waited outside, under the intense heat of the sun, for me to complete the exam. When the bell rang and the exam finished, I went outside and she hugged me, holding me tight. I saw a bottle in her hand; it was a beverage she had bought me. I was very thirsty and started drinking it. The drink was soothing and cool, but her hug was even more refreshing. I looked at her face, and I saw her sweat pouring down. I gave her the bottle immediately and asked her to please drink. "You drink, my son. I am not thirsty," she replied. This was her fourth lie.

After my father passed away, my mother lived the life of a lonely widow and mother. The responsibility of taking care of the house and family fell on her shoulders alone. She was in charge of furnishing all of our needs, and life became more complicated. We started suffering from hunger. Fortunately, my uncle was a kind man who lived next door, so he used to send us food. When the neighbors saw our situation, they advised my mother to get married to someone who could support us financially. After all, she was still young. However, my mother refused. "I do not need love," she said. This was her fifth lie.

After I graduated from university and got a good job, I thought it was finally the right time for my mother to retire, stay home, and leave the financial responsibility of the house to me. By then, she was very weak and could not walk from one house to another as a salesperson. Instead, every morning she went to the market where she would spread a blanket upon which she would sell produce. When she refused to quit, I allocated part of my salary to her. But she refused to take it and said, "My son, keep your money for yourself; I have enough." This was her sixth lie.

While I was working, I continued studying. I earned my master's degree and was promoted. A German company that I worked for gave me the opportunity to transfer to their headquarters in Germany. I was so excited; I started dreaming of a new beginning and a happy life to follow. After flying there for a visit and making all of my arrangements, I asked my mother to come and live with me. However, she refused because she did not want to trouble me. She said, "Son, I would not know how to live a fancy life." This was her seventh lie.

My mother grew old and was diagnosed with cancer. I needed to be next to her during her illness. Who else would take care of her? I dropped everything and flew back immediately to be at her bedside. Once I arrived, I found her lying in bed after the surgery. When she saw me, she tried to smile. My heart tore apart as I realized how frail and sick she had become. She was not the mother I knew. I cried, and she tried to calm me, saying, "Do not cry; I am not in pain." This was her eighth lie.

After saying this, she closed her eyes and never opened them again.

To all who are blessed by the presence of a mother in their life, take care of this blessing before you taste the sadness of losing it.

And to those who have lost their loving mothers, never forget how she suffered for your sake. And never forget her in your prayers.

Lessons Learned:

1. **Sacrifice and Selflessness**
    We often hear about the sacrifices that a mother makes for her children, and we have witnessed it ourselves as well. A mother gives without asking for anything in return. She is like an unknown soldier, giving with love and dedication, never seeking to be mentioned. The Quran describes one who does not understand and appreciate sacrifice as *Jabbar* (cold-hearted), and as *Shaqi* (one who misses the blessings of this life and the hereafter). Our Prophet Jesus (PBUH) asked God to help him to be righteous toward his mother. The Quran describes Jesus as saying, "*And (God made me) dutiful to my mother, and He has not made me a wretched tyrant.*"[5] Be among the people who value the sacrifices of one's mother, drawing closer to God through that appreciation; avoid ungratefulness, which deprives one from the reward gained by caring for one's mother.

2. **A Healthy Mind Originates in a Healthy Body**
    This wise mother understood her financial responsibilities and realized that she was having difficulty in buying healthy food for her son. She did not neglect her responsibilities or blame her husband or circumstances; instead she looked for suitable alternatives, like fishing in the river. The fish helped her son maintain a healthy body and mind. A sound mind comes from a sound body. One should strive to be like this mother. Even if we have limited means, we should still feed our children foods that will benefit their minds and bodies, instead of harmful

---

[5] [Maryam:32]

foods that end up hurting them much more than it benefits them.

3. **The Upper Hand Is Better Than the Lower Hand**
This wise woman wanted to raise her son with strong values, in this case living by lawful (*halal*) earnings, acquired through hard work. One should seek out work to earn money, not beg and seek handouts. According to Al-Bukhari, Prophet Muhammad (PBUH) said, "*Nobody has ever eaten a better meal than that which was earned by working with his own hands. Prophet David (PBUH) used to eat from the earnings of his manual labor.*"[6] Although she could have asked for money, the mother preferred to earn it through her own hard work. By doing so, she set an example of strong character and dignity for her son. She taught him to work hard to earn a living for himself, rather than to display weakness, wait for handouts, or limit himself to asking for charity.

4. **Encouragement and Prayer Are Essential Pillars of Success**
We can see how this wise mother gave encouragement and emotional support to her son by going with him to his exam, praying for his success, and being next to him through his tough moments. She gave him a sense of tranquility, support, and mercy, and provided a nurturing environment in which he could achieve. She knew the greatness of God, who is the Responder. As God said in the Quran, "*And your Lord says, 'Call upon Me; I will respond to you ...*'"[7]

---

[6] Narrated by Bukhari.
[7] [Ghafir:60]

14

5. **Investing in One's Children is the Best Investment**
   This mother refused money and a prosperous life in favor of a yet more important investment in her son. She wanted him to be well-educated and a benefit to his community. To this mother, her son's education was worth everything and was more valuable than other materialistic purchases that would never last. One must consider intellectual investments rather than material ones.

6. **Overcome Adversity to Meet One's Goals**
   This mother had a goal, which was to help her son achieve academic success. She focused all of her efforts on the care of her son, and she sacrificed her personal rights and needs in order to overcome their difficulties. She even abandoned finding love for herself by rejecting the possibility of getting remarried. She refused to take a portion of her son's salary that would have eased her circumstances, and she declined the offer of a luxurious lifestyle that awaited her in Germany. She sacrificed every worldly comfort to ensure that her son would achieve his goals. She did so to safeguard her son's future, and she refused to be an obstacle in his path to success.

7. **Success Is the Greatest Cure for Pain and Suffering**
   We can see the suffering and sacrifices of this mother. We might ask ourselves why she endured until the very last moment and refused to share her problems with her son. The answer is that her main objective was for her son to achieve his goals. This was the ultimate relief for her pain and suffering. She did her part to ensure that a promising future for her son was carefully designed, planned, and built, thereby focusing her energy and ignoring her own pain. She was like the winner of a race; although exhausted, the joy of victory outweighed underlying

fatigue, soreness, and pain. How many of us sacrifice for someone else's success? And how many of us consider the success of others as our own personal achievement?

8. **The Mutual Care of Mother and Child**

The reader of this story sees a realistic, contemporary image of a righteous parent caring for her child. She does everything to please him without requesting anything in return. How, then, should children care for their parents? And how can children begin to repay their parents to whom they are indebted for their incredible sacrifices? Kindness toward parents should truly be a high priority for every child, especially with the knowledge that righteousness toward parents draws us closer to God. Prophet Muhammad (PBUH) taught that good treatment toward parents is among the greatest acts of goodness one can perform, comparable in significance to both the worship of God in prayer and to the exertion in the path of righteousness, *Jihad*.

Abdullah Ibn Mas'ud asked Prophet Muhammad (PBUH), "*Which deed is most beloved to God?*" Prophet Muhammad (PBUH) replied, "*Prayer on time.*"

"*Which one is next?*" Abdullah then asked. Prophet Muhammad (PBUH) answered, "*Kindness to parents.*"

Abdullah asked one final time, "*Which one after that?*"

Prophet Muhammad (PBUH) concluded, "*Jihad in the way of God.*"

It was told that Ali Ibn Al-Hussain Zayn Al-'Abidin did not like to eat with his mother at the same table. When he was asked why, he replied, "I am afraid that my hand would grasp a portion of food that her eye was watching, thereby dishonoring her."

— 3 —

Kindness to Parents
The Story of 'Uwais Al-Qarni [8]

One day, while sitting with his good friend and companion, 'Umar Ibn Al-Khattab, Prophet Muhammad (PBUH) told 'Umar about Uwais al-Qarni whom the Prophet (PBUH) had never met. Uwais was from a town called Qarn in Yemen, from a tribe known as Murad, he explained. Uwais' father died, and so he was considered an orphaned child. He lived alone with his mother, to whom he was very obedient. Uwais had a skin disease known as leprosy, and he prayed to God for a cure. The Prophet (PBUH) mentioned that Uwais' prayers were answered and he was cured, except for a mark on his arm in the shape of a coin. Years later, Uwais would become known as the Master of the Followers (*Tabi'een*), the

---

[8] Hadith narrated by Muslim, from 'Umar Ibn Al-Khattab, from Tabaqaat Ibn Saad.

first generation of Muslims who had never met the Prophet (PBUH). Prophet Muhammad (PBUH) told 'Umar that if he was ever able to meet Uwais, he should request Uwais to ask God for Umar's forgiveness.

'Umar kept the words of Prophet Muhammad (PBUH) in his heart, and he never forgot his mention of the blessed man. When 'Umar became the Caliph, every year he would ask the pilgrims who arrived in Mecca from Yemen about Uwais. "Is Uwais Al-Qarni among you?" When they answered 'No', he would ask, "How is he doing?" The answers were consistent, that he had few belongings and wore shabby clothes. This always upset 'Umar to hear that Uwais lived in unfavorable circumstances. 'Umar responded, "May God be merciful to you, for the Messenger of God (PBUH) mentioned him. If you are able to, request from him to ask for God's forgiveness on your behalf."

'Umar continued to ask the pilgrims about Uwais year after year and he would always hear the same report. At long last, one year Uwais was finally among the travelers from Yemen who were in Mecca to make pilgrimage (*Hajj*). Umar hoped he had finally found Uwais, but he needed to be sure of his identity. He began to ask him some questions.

"What is your name?" asked 'Umar Ibn Al-Khattab.

"My name is Uwais," answered Uwais.

"What city are you from in Yemen?" asked 'Umar Ibn Al-Khattab.

"I am from the city of Qarn," answered Uwais.

"Which tribe are you from?" asked 'Umar.

"I am from the tribe of Murad," replied Uwais.

"How is your father?" asked 'Umar Ibn Al-Khattab.

"My father passed away long ago and my mother lives with me," answered Uwais.

"How do you treat your mother?" asked 'Umar, regarding the crucial matter that surely warranted God's tremendous favor upon Uwais.

"I try to treat her with kindness," answered Uwais.

"Have you ever been ill?" asked 'Umar Ibn Al-Khattab.

"Yes, I was afflicted with leprosy, but after I made supplication (*duaa*), God cured me from the disease," answered Uwais.

"Do you have anything remaining from your disease?" asked 'Umar Ibn Al-Khattab.

"Yes I do. I have a mark shaped like a coin," answered Uwais, as he pulled up his sleeve to show 'Umar his scar.

Upon seeing the scar, 'Umar hugged Uwais with all his might, and exclaimed, "You are the one whom the Messenger of God (PBUH) mentioned! Please ask God for my forgiveness!"

Uwais was shocked. He wondered, how could the Caliph want me, a simple and poor shepherd, to ask God's forgiveness on behalf of the Caliph?! Bewildered, Uwais replied, "How can I ask God to forgive you, Oh Leader of the Faithful, when the Messenger of God (PBUH) has already ascertained that you will be in Paradise?"

'Umar continued to plead with Uwais, insisting that he must grant his request, until Uwais finally agreed and prayed for 'Umar's forgiveness. Content, 'Umar then asked Uwais where he planned to go upon completing the pilgrimage.

Uwais answered, "I am going to a town called Kufa in Iraq."

'Umar asked, "Shall I write to the magistrate of Iraq on your behalf?"

Uwais immediately refused and said, "I swear, oh Leader of the Faithful, you should not do so. Leave me to go among the people without any special care; that is what I would love most." He then departed.

Lessons Learned:

1. **Being Honored**
   Prophet Muhammad (PBUH) did not honor Uwais
   by mentioning him to his companions for being
   extra zealous, but for honoring his mother and being
   obedient to her. How many of us show exceptional
   treatment to our parents? How many of us would
   like to receive this honor in the hereafter? Whoever
   hopes to reach a similar rank should be good to their
   parents, for along with their good treatment comes
   obedience, worship, blessings, and a reward that
   never ends.

2. **The Companions Sought Out Actions to Draw
   Them Closer to God**
   Despite 'Umar Ibn Al-Khattab's immense
   responsibility as leader of the Muslims, and even
   though he had already been promised heaven, he
   did not cease looking for more ways to reap reward.
   He strove to find ways to get closer to God, and he
   clung to the Prophet's (PBUH) words and advice.
   Every year, 'Umar Ibn Al-Khattab tried to find Uwais
   to ask for his supplication on his behalf. He knew
   that the paths to righteousness are numerous, and
   he wanted to try a variety of avenues so that perhaps
   one path might bring him success. Sometimes we
   find it difficult to be steadfast in our duties to God,
   including following the example of our Prophet
   (PBUH). Perseverance is crucial; let us follow the
   steps of our early Caliph 'Umar Ibn Al-Khattab and
   learn from his steadfastness.

3. **The Greatness of the Reward for Obeying One's Parents**

God is Merciful. He honored Uwais by curing him from a chronic illness. He then further honored him by mentioning him, so that we may still know of him today. He was honored yet again by having his supplications (*duaa*) answered and accepted. All of this was because he was good to his mother.

4. **Being Sincere in One's Work and Not Seeking Fame**

When Uwais learned that God had honored him by accepting the prayers he made, he did not seek great fame, status, or rank. He wanted to remain an average person without being given any distinction. All he wanted was to be honored and distinguished in the hereafter.

5. **Being Humble and Poor Did Not Prevent Uwais from Being Distinguished**

Although Uwais was poor and modest, he did not allow the misfortunes in his life to affect his duties to God. Instead of dwelling on the fact that he was disadvantaged, he used his energy to take care of his widowed mother, intent on following God's orders. Let us renew our intentions and not dwell on the misfortunes of this world. Once God raised his status and honored him by answering his supplication (*duaa*), Uwais still did not become arrogant, or even allow himself to be distinguished from other people. Instead, he humbly turned to God out of gratitude for the favors He bestowed upon him, and for the blessings that could never be counted or quantified.

6. **Using Wisdom and Manners When Seeking Out Information**

The careful way in which 'Umar Ibn Al-Khattab approached Uwais to confirm that he was indeed the one whom the Prophet (PBUH) had recognized sets a true example. Umar's short and gradual questions illustrate the manners and wisdom of the Caliph. He did not bombard, interrogate, or overwhelm Uwais. If we practice wisdom and use the best manners, we will find what we seek.

"And We have commanded man (to care) for his parents. His mother carried him (increasing her) in weakness upon weakness, and his weaning is in two years. Be grateful to Me and to your parents; to Me is the (final) destination. But if they endeavor to make you associate with Me that of which you have no knowledge, do not obey them but accompany them in (this) world with appropriate kindness and follow the way of those who turn back to Me (in repentance). Then to Me will be your return, and I will inform you about what you used to do."

[Luqman:14–15]

— 4 —
Dear to God, Dutiful to Parents
My Companion in Paradise[9]

Prophet Moses (PBUH) asked God Almighty, "Oh God, who will be my friend in Paradise?"

God sent His revelation to Prophet Moses and said, "Oh Moses, the first man who will pass by you along this path will be your friend in Paradise."

Not long afterward, a man came along the path and passed by Prophet Moses (PBUH). He decided to follow the man. Intrigued, Prophet Moses (PBUH) wanted to understand what the man had accomplished in order to be so honored as to have earned the friendship of a prophet in Paradise.

---
[9] Dalil Al-Sa'ileen, pg. 103, by Anas Ismail Abu Dawud.

Prophet Moses (PBUH) continued to follow him until they reached a house. The man entered the home and sat before an elderly woman. He took out some meat and grilled it. He then fed her, putting the cooked meat in her mouth. Next, the man put water in her mouth to drink. He left soon after.

Moses (PBUH) approached the man and asked, "By God, who is this woman?"

The man did not yet know who was addressing him. He answered, "She is my mother."

Prophet Moses (PBUH) asked him, "What does she ask from God for you?"

The man replied, "She makes one supplication (*duaa*) for me, never changing it."

Moses (PBUH) asked, "What does she say in her supplication (*duaa*)?"

The man said, "She says, 'Oh God, take my son to Paradise with Moses of Imran.'"

Moses (PBUH) replied, "Rejoice, for God has answered your mother's prayers. I am Moses of Imran, and you will be my friend in Paradise, God willing!"

Therefore, the man's success was due to the blessing of his mother's supplication (*duaa*), for parents' prayers made for their children are always answered.

Lessons Learned:

1. **Manners in Posing Questions**
    Asking questions is a beneficial habit. Prophet Moses
    (PBUH) used to seek knowledge, probing so that he
    might learn not only about his life, but also details
    of the hereafter. He did not, however, ask questions
    in order to argue or to be unyielding in his opinion.
    We should ask questions for the sake of gaining
    knowledge we can then put into practice, not to be
    argumentative or to try to prove others wrong. After
    all, God knows best.

2. **The Great Reward of Being Righteous to Parents**
    Many of us do not really understand the great reward
    of treating our parents with goodness. God says,
    *"Worship God and associate nothing with Him, and do
    good to parents."*[10] We can see that God linked the act
    of honoring one's parents with the act of worshipping
    God. A parent's love is part of the love God shows
    us. Grow close to God by worshipping Him and by
    kindly caring for your parents. In this way, success
    will be achieved through God's satisfactions, God
    willing.

3. **The Characteristic of the Righteousness**
    The man applied a critical rule regarding the
    treatment of parents: hasten to satisfy their needs
    before they ever need to come ask for assistance.
    The man fed his mother and gave her water before
    he even ate anything for himself. Unfortunately, this
    is a great departure from how many children treat
    their parents today. Children often disrespect their
    parents by raising their voices, being argumentative,
    and sometimes even blaming them for their own

---

[10] [Al-Nisaa:36]

mistakes. Fear God in one's treatment of parents and show them the respect they deserve; avoid their displeasure before it is too late.

4. **The Prayers of Parents are Answered**
   Prophet Muhammad (PBUH) said, "*Three prayers are surely answered: the supplication of the oppressed, the supplication of the traveler, and the supplication of the father for his son.*"[11] The mother had nothing to give her son except supplication. This was actually more precious than anything she could have given him materially. We should increase our good deeds in order to receive the benefit of our parents' accepted prayers for us, and we will see the resulting blessings that will come.

5. **The Company of the Prophets and the Admission into Paradise**
   This man was honored by two things: The first was the entry into Paradise, and the second was the elevation to the rank among the prophets in Paradise. Both were due to his righteous treatment of his mother. Similarly, in the time of Prophet Muhammad (PBUH), it was narrated that Mu'awiyah Ibn Jahimah came to Muhammad (PBUH) to take his advice regarding entering a battle and participating in *jihad*. The Prophet (PBUH) asked him, "*Do you have a mother?*"
   Mu'awiyah Ibn Jahimah said, "Yes." The Prophet replied, "*Stay with her, because Paradise lies beneath her feet.*"[12] Therefore, if you want to enter Paradise and have the friendship of the prophets, obey your parents and treat them well.

---

[11] Narrated by Ibn Majah.
[12] Narrated by Al-Nisa'i and Ahmad.

6. Shall Goodness Be Rewarded with Anything But Goodness?

Our mothers gave birth to us, raised us, stayed up at night to care for us, served us in our early years, and wished for us goodness and success throughout adulthood. Do they not deserve that we remain at their sides as they become old and frail? God, likewise, deserves that we reciprocate goodness toward Him for all His kindness to us. Therefore, do not be among those who reward goodness with neglect; be wise, so that we may win in this life and in the hereafter, God willing.

"And decree for us in this world (that which is) good and (also) in the Hereafter; indeed, we have turned back to You.' (God) said, 'My punishment - I afflict with it whom I will, but My mercy encompasses all things.' So I will decree it (especially) for those who fear Me and pay alms (zakah) and those who believe in Our verses."

[Al-A'raf:156]

— 5 —

God Is the Merciful

The Man Who Worshipped God for Five-Hundred Years[13]

Jabir Ibn Abdullah (may God be pleased with him) reported that the Prophet Muhammad (PBUH) came to him and some companions and said, "My dear and beloved friend (angel) Gabriel came to me just now and said, 'Oh Muhammad, by He who has sent you with truth, there is a servant of God who has worshipped Him continuously for five-hundred years. He was living on top of a mountain with the dimensions of thirty arm's-lengths by thirty arm's-lengths, surrounded by the sea, four-thousand leagues in every direction. Although it was surrounded by salty water, God caused a stream of fresh water to flow at the base of the mountain for him.'"

---

[13] Hadith, narrated from a sound chain (*sahih*), mentioned in Shifa' al-Alil, Volume 1, pg. 356, by Ibn Qayyim.

The Prophet (PBUH) continued, sharing Gabriel's words, "'God also made a pomegranate tree grow that produced one pomegranate every day which would feed the man for the day. Every evening the man would use the fresh water to make ablution (*wudu*), and would pick the pomegranate to eat.'"

The Prophet (PBUH) added, "'The man would then stand to pray, and he would ask of God to take his soul while he was in a state of prostration, and that nothing on earth or anything beyond would corrupt him.'"

God accepted his supplication. Every time Gabriel came down to earth, he found the man in prostration to God. Gabriel said that, on the Day of Judgment, the man will stand before his Lord and God will say of him, "Take my servant to Paradise out of My mercy." The man will respond, "No, rather through my deeds," insisting that he should enter Paradise through the good deeds and acts of devotion that he had performed during his lifetime.

Again, God will say, "Take my servant to Paradise out of My mercy," and again, the man will say, "No, rather through my deeds," adamant to enter Paradise by the merit of his deeds alone.

For a third time, God will repeat, "Take my servant to Paradise out of My mercy," and for a final time, the man will reply, "No, rather through my deeds," persisting in his desire to have the merit of his actions weighed alone to carry him into Paradise.

God will then order the angels, "Measure the favors bestowed upon my servant in comparison to his deeds." It will be determined that when the gift of eyesight is compared to the five-hundred years of worship, the blessing of his eyesight will yet outweigh his deeds.

God will order the angels, "Take my servant to the hellfire." He will be dragged toward the hellfire. With his scales weighing against the man's favor, he will finally plead, "Oh God, allow me to enter Paradise through Your mercy alone!"

God will say, "Return him." Once the man is in front of him, God will ask him, "Who created you, my servant, when you were nonexistent?" The man will reply, "You, my Lord." God will then ask, "Was that from you or out of My mercy?" The man will reply. "Only out of Your mercy."

God will then ask, "Who granted you the strength to worship for five-hundred years?" The servant will respond, "You, my Lord." God will continue to ask, "Who placed you on the mountain in the middle of an abyss and who separated fresh water for you from the saltwater? And (who) produced a pomegranate for you every night when it should grow just once a year? When you asked Me to take your soul in the state of prostration, did I do that for you?"

The man will humbly reply, "You did, my Lord."

God will then say, "All this happened due to My mercy and you will enter Paradise only, too, out of My mercy. Take My servant to Paradise. You were a devout worshipper, My servant." Then, God will allow him to enter Paradise.

Then Gabriel said to Muhammad (PBUH), "Indeed all matters come about only due to the mercy of God."

Lessons Learned:

1. **Do Not Overlook Acts of Worship**
   The Prophet (PBUH) wanted to teach the
   companions an important lesson; even though they
   worked to perfect the worship of God, there were yet
   other people before them who worshipped God even
   more. Do not be deluded into thinking one is doing
   God a favor by worshipping Him. We should always
   remain sincere in our devotion to God.

2. **Obedience to God Brings Blessings in This World
   and the Next**
   God granted this devout worshipper many blessings
   in his lifetime, including fresh spring water, the
   pomegranate tree, and so much more than could ever
   be quantified. Additionally, for a blessed hereafter,
   God granted him death while in prostration, a
   good end to his life. When this happens, it implies
   the anticipation that one shall enter Paradise, God
   willing.

3. **Worship God Through Remembrance and
   Gratitude for His Blessings**
   Mankind often forgets the favors bestowed upon
   him by God, so remember and reflect daily upon the
   vastness of your own God-given blessings. Never
   be deluded into thinking that one's achievements
   have been earned through wealth, thought, or deed;
   surely, even the things for which you have worked are
   merely gifts from God Almighty. So be thankful to
   God through humble gratitude.

4. **Feel Remorse and Do Not Persist in Errors**
   Despite the perfection of his devotion, the
   worshipper persists to argue with God which almost
   leads him to perish and enter the hellfire. Do not

argue with those who are more knowledgeable for it leads to inevitable regret, as witnessed by this worshipper.

5. **Advancement Is Only Out of God's Mercy**
   Get closer to God by perfecting acts of devotion with sincerity and, God willing, He will accept good deeds and facilitate the entrance into Paradise through His mercy.

"And when Abraham said, 'My Lord, show me how You give life to the dead.' (God) said, 'Have you not believed?' He said, 'Yes, but (I ask) only that my heart may be satisfied.' (God) said, 'Take four birds and tame them. Then (after slaughtering them) put on each hill a portion of them; then call them - they will come (flying) to you in haste. And know that God is Exalted in Might and Wise.'"

[Al-Baqarah:260]

— 6 —
God, the Giver of Life
The Story of Ezra ('Uzair) [14]

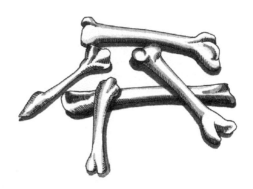

Many years had passed, and the Israelites in Palestine had strayed from their religion. After they had neglected the Torah, forgetting much of its verses and teachings, God wanted to renew their faith. He sent them Ezra ('Uzair), who was a pious man.

God commanded Ezra to go to a designated town in order to remind and guide the people about God. He commenced his journey, but when he arrived, he was astonished to find it had been utterly destroyed and abandoned. It was completely deserted, fallen into ruin with bones scattered about. Ezra stood there alone wondering, "*How will God bring this town*

---

[14] Quran [Al-Baqarah:259], Summary of Tafsir (Exegesis) of Imam Ismail Ibn Kathir, volume 1, pg. 421-422.

to life after its death?"[15]

Suddenly, God took the soul of Ezra, bringing his own death. One-hundred years passed, then God brought Ezra back to life. He sent Ezra an angel in the form of a human. The angel asked him, *"How long have you remained here?"*[16]

Ezra responded, *"I have remained a day, or part of a day."*[17]

The angel cried, *"You have actually remained here for one-hundred years. Look at your food and your drink. It has not changed with time. And cast your eyes upon your donkey. We will make you a sign for your people."*[18] Indeed, he saw that the food that he had left next to him remained just as he had left it, without rotting or changing in appearance, taste, or smell. Yet, his donkey had since died and all that was left were the bones of its skeleton.

Then before his own eyes, Ezra saw a truly wondrous thing: the bones started moving until the skeleton was arranged into the form of a donkey. Miraculously, the skeleton was then covered with flesh, then skin, then hair. God gave life to the donkey before Ezra's very own eyes. The angel then said, *"Look at the bones (of this donkey), how We raised them and then We covered them with flesh."*[19]

Ezra was in awe as he exclaimed, *"I know that God has power over all things!"*[20] Indeed, how magnificent was this incredible miracle of God.

---

[15] [Al-Baqarah:259]
[16] [Al-Baqarah:259]
[17] [Al-Baqarah:259]
[18] [Al-Baqarah:259]
[19] [Al-Baqarah:259]
[20] [Al-Baqarah:259]

Ezra then ventured into town and found it bustling, crowded with people. It was no longer the uninhabited, abandoned town he had come to just before his slumber. He approached those around him, asking, "Do you know of a man named Ezra?"

Those he asked replied, "Yes, we know of him, but he died a century ago."

He told them, "I am Ezra!" revealing his identity to those around him. The inhabitants of the town found his story very difficult to believe, so they brought an elderly woman to come describe Ezra as she remembered him. The woman's description gave the townspeople clear confirmation that the man before them was indeed Ezra.

Upon verifying Ezra's identity, all of the people accepted him and his message. He began to teach the Torah. The townspeople adhered to his teachings and believed in the religion sent to them by God. They loved and honored him dearly, and revered him for the miraculous event that had transpired.

Unfortunately, the inhabitants of the town became extremely enamored with Ezra. Over time, the people altered his message out of their devotion to him. They even declared that he was divine. Over generations, their reverence of him was distorted into the worship of him. Eventually, they even called Ezra the son of God. God says in the Quran, "*The Jews proclaimed, ' Ezra is the son of God ... '*"[21] Some still believe today that Ezra is the son of God. May God keep us steadfast and lead us to the right path.

---

[21] [Al-Tawba:30]

Lessons Learned:

1. **God's Will and Wisdom**
   God asked Ezra to go to the town, but Ezra could
   not understand why God would possibly send him
   to the uninhabited town to teach its nonexistent
   citizens. But God wanted to make his faith firm, and
   to return him to the town after one-hundred years.
   The inhabitants would then witness this miracle
   with complete certainty and believe in the message
   without doubt. Out of God's wisdom, this was best
   for him and his people.

2. **Having Certainty That God Has Power Over All
   Things, Even Life and Death**
   Never despair or deem circumstances as impossible.
   Nothing is impossible for God, including reviving
   bones after they have deteriorated. Certainly, then,
   we should never think that it is impossible for God to
   grant us what we most desire.

3. **Teaching Through Proof**
   God Almighty strengthened Ezra's faith by showing
   him His power. Seeing with his own two eyes the
   arrangement of the donkey's bones that were then
   covered with flesh, skin, and hair was deemed more
   convincing than words alone. Actions speak louder
   than words.

4. **The Foundation of Learning is Revival**
   When Ezra went to the people and started teaching
   them the lessons of the Torah, he was reviving their
   neglected faith. Finding new methods to convey the
   unchanging message is a critical way to bring revival
   of faith to the masses, particularly when teaching
   religious matters.

5. **Excessive Infatuation Leads to Deviation**
    God has forbidden us from showing divine love
    toward the prophets and the righteous; this ruling
    extends to all those who are beloved, whether a
    wife, a husband, or even a pious man or woman.
    Displaying extreme love and infatuation toward
    humans is a deviation from God's guidance, breaks
    His divine laws, and leads to idolatry, which can lead
    one to perish.

"Oh you who believe, fasting is prescribed for you as it was prescribed for those before you, so that you may become righteous."

[Al-Baqarah:183]

— 7 —

Fasting and Higher Consciousness[22]

On the very day that God saved the Children of Israel (*Bani Israil*) from Pharaoh and his army by drowning them in the Red Sea, Prophet Moses (PBUH) made a great decision; he must venture to Mount Sinai (*Tur*) in hope of receiving guidance from God to help lead his people. Indeed, this journey resulted in the revelation of the sacred book known as the Torah (*Tawrat*).

The Children of Israel could not endure the hardships of both the long duration and the strenuous nature of the trip. Therefore, Moses (PBUH) asked his brother, Prophet Aaron (*Harun*, PBUH) to remain and lead the six-hundred-

---

[22] Maa Al-Anbiyaa'; Qisas Al-Quran Al-Karim, pg. 243-244, by 'Afif Abdullah Tabarah.

thousand followers. By doing so, he could help to keep them steadfast and to guide them on God's path.

After a long journey, Prophet Moses (PBUH) finally arrived at Mount Sinai. But before God revealed the information that Moses (PBUH) sought, he had to pass yet another test. Moses (PBUH) was instructed to stay on Mount Sinai and fast for thirty days. This was a means to come closer to God as a yet more devoted servant. He patiently fasted day after day.

When Moses (PBUH) had finally completed this momentous undertaking, God requested that he fast an additional ten days to ensure that he had fully achieved the completion and perfection of his act of worship. Moses (PBUH) devoted himself wholly to the worship of God, and thus rose to a level never before achieved.

After the completion of the forty days, Prophet Moses (PBUH) reached such a high degree of piety that God granted him an incredible privilege, unique to him alone. God spoke to Prophet Moses (PBUH) directly. He was the only human to ever be given this extraordinary honor.

In his newly elevated rank, Prophet Moses (PBUH) now yearned for God to reveal Himself so that He could be seen. Moses (PBUH) asked God to show Himself. However, God responded, "*You will not see Me, but look at the mountain; if it should remain in place, then you will see Me.*"[23] In direct response to God's statement, the Mountain began to crumble. It continued to do so until it had completely collapsed and its remnants lay flat upon the ground.

Upon witnessing this remarkable event, Prophet Moses

---

[23] [Al-A'raf:143]

45

(PBUH) fell unconscious, shocked by the grandness of God's presence. When he awoke, he turned to God in repentance and pledged that he was the first true believer in his time. God answered him:

" ... 'O Moses, I have chosen you over the people with My messages and My words (to you). So take what I have given you and be among the grateful.' And We wrote for him on the tablets of all things - instruction and explanation for all things, (saying), 'Take them with determination and order your people to take the best of it. I will show you the home of the defiantly disobedient.'"[24]

---

[24] [Al-A'raf:144-145]

Lessons Learned:

1. **Fasting Is an Act of Worship That Prepares One for Piety**
   God teaches us that in order to gain piety, a person must first worship God through acts of devotion, such as fasting. Prophet Moses (PBUH) did not just fast one day; he fasted thirty days and then an additional ten in order to learn how to be truly patient through hunger and thirst. He stood alone in worship in front of God. This fast purified Moses (PBUH) and raised him in rank. By patiently dismissing hunger and thirst from his mind to obey God for forty days, he was able to attain an immense amount of piety achieved by only a select few.
   For Muslims, God made the fasting of the month of Ramadan as a means to erase sins committed throughout the year, from one Ramadan to the next. However, God also created fasting as a means of purification and as a way to become elevated to a true state of God-consciousness.

2. **Passing Hardships Brings About Blessings**
   After Moses (PBUH) patiently passed his hardship, he was rewarded with God's book, the Torah (*Tawrat*). He also received advice from God about how to best use this book as a warning to his people of His punishment if they chose to disobey Him.

3. **Prophets Are Human and Possess Human Emotions**
   Like any human, Moses (PBUH) felt well-accomplished for having had the willpower to overcome desire through fasting and, therefore, passing his test. When he asked to see God, Moses

(PBUH) was inquiring out of both curiosity and eagerness to see his Lord after hearing His voice. Our Creator knows our feelings and how we handle rejection. Out of consideration for Moses (PBUH), God answered Moses' (PBUH) request by showing him that seeing God is beyond the capacity of any earthly creation. Seeing Him would only destroy him as it had leveled the mountain. God conveyed this message to Moses (PBUH) in a considerate way so as to not diminish his feeling of accomplishment.

4. **Do Not Be Afraid to Ask Questions**
   Without asking questions we will never receive answers, and this will leave us deprived of valuable knowledge. When we are without answers, we are without knowledge. Questions and curiosity are the very keys to enlightenment, and without them we will never learn.
   Prophet Moses (PBUH) was neither too afraid nor too shy to ask God to see Him. Furthermore, we should never be shy to ask God for anything our hearts desire, just as Moses (PBUH) did. Although God did not grant him his request, Moses was still presented with an amazing display of God's greatness. Through this, we all learn the lesson that God is far too great for us to behold. God loves us to ask of Him, and we only benefit by asking God for everything we could ever want.

"Indeed, anyone who fasts for one day for the sake of God, God will keep his face away from the hellfire by the distance covered over a journey of seventy years."

Prophet Muhammad (PBUH)
Reported by Abu Sa'id Al-Khudri

— 8 —
The Reward for the Fasting[25]

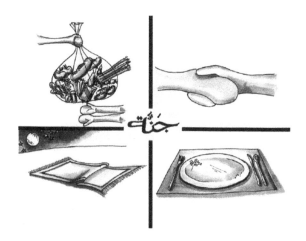

The Prophet Muhammad (PBUH) loved to teach his companions about Islam and increase their love for their faith. One day, as some companions were sitting with the Prophet (PBUH), he asked, "Would you like me to tell you about the rooms in Paradise?"

The companions immediately prompted him to share his invaluable description. The Prophet (PBUH) smiled and began to depict one particular room in Heaven to his companions. As he began the remarkable description, the companions listening could have perhaps imagined it as a crystal ball; one can see what is inside from the outside. The

---

[25] Hadith narrated by Al-Hasan from Jabir, cited by Abu Na'im, referenced from Ihya' Ulum Al-Din, Volume 4, Imam Al-Ghazali.

colors are magnificent, beyond one's imagination. The room is filled with things that no eye has ever seen, and no ear has ever heard. The thought of such a place has never crossed any living person's mind before. Such a room in Heaven encompasses things a normal human mind could never imagine: they have never been seen, tasted, or felt before.

Astounded by the incredible description, one of the companions, Jabir, eagerly asked, "For whom is this special room prepared?"

The Prophet (PBUH) replied, "God has prepared it for those who feed others generously, who greet by saying 'salaam' to those whom they know and those whom they do not know, who fast continuously, and who stand in prayer at night when people are sleeping."

Jabir was distraught, and said, "Our dear Prophet, who can really do all of these things?" He wondered, who could really fast every day? Who could greet all those whom he may know, but also those whom he may not know? Who could feed the poor and needy daily? It appeared to be much too difficult. Who could really accomplish all of this?

The Prophet (PBUH) looked at Jabir kindly and said, "My nation (ummah) can do so, Oh Jabir, and I shall explain how." He explained that by saying 'salaam,' he meant stating a mere 'assalamu alaikum' and showing a simple smile to everyone one sees would suffice. One could couple the 'salaam' with a strong hand shake if one knows the person being greeted. This helps to give the reassurance that Muslims are indeed peaceful and are genuinely caring toward others.

Jabir began to understand a little better as the Prophet (PBUH) continued. He explained that by feeding the poor, he did not mean feeding all of the poor. What was meant was rather to feed one's family first. Any extra could then feed neighbors and, beyond that, the poor and needy. If one does not have enough to feed all of these people, then feeding one's family would suffice.

Jabir's face changed, listening anxiously as he began to understand that it was indeed achievable to enter the described room in Paradise. The Prophet (PBUH) continued to explain that the requirement was not to fast every day. Fasting the month of Ramadan in addition to fasting three days from every month would be rewarded as if one fasted the full year.

All the companions' faces were now beaming, anxious to begin what the Prophet (PBUH) advised them to do. The Prophet (PBUH) continued his explanation, clarifying that it was indeed not as hard as they thought. As for standing in prayer at night when others were sleeping, he explained that praying the morning prayer (*fajr*) and the evening prayer (*isha*) with a group is as if one stayed up praying all night.

All of the companions were extremely grateful to the Prophet (PBUH) for simplifying the hadith in a way that they could understand and realistically achieve. He inspired them and helped them to understand how easily this could be done. May God guide us all to the straight path and give us opportunities to please Him so that we may enter this beautiful room in Paradise!

Lessons Learned:

1. **Taking Advantage of the Learning Environment and the Art of Starting Conversations**
We learn from our Prophet (PBUH) the way in which he taught his companions about Islam. The Prophet (PBUH) began with a question to which nobody knew the answer. He did this to gain everyone's attention and prompt their intrigue. He kept them in suspense for the answer. Then, he tried his best to simplify the message so that they could implement it in their everyday lives.

2. **Explaining the Reward Before the Deeds**
This related story (*hadith*) begins with the description of a room in Paradise and how beautiful it is. The reader is left in suspense as one learns that such a room in Paradise holds things that are beyond one's greatest imagination. Even the reader contemplates the description and is eager to learn how to earn the privilege to enter. The Prophet (PBUH) strategically told of the great reward first, followed by how to realistically achieve it.

3. **Simple and Easy**
The Prophet (PBUH) made his companions understand that entering Paradise is an achievable accomplishment, one that any of them could do. Additionally, entering this special room in Paradise is easy for one who completes four basic things. He paid close attention to keep everything simplified, described in a way that everyone could easily comprehend.

4. **Repeating Without Complicating**
We learn from the Prophet (PBUH) a great way to repeat and further explain concepts to make them

clear. Sometimes listeners become confused when speakers give explanations that are too elaborate or difficult. In addition, speakers sometimes express annoyance when those listening ask for clarification. The Prophet (PBUH) kindly took his time to further explain his point in a simple, uncomplicated, and non-condescending way.

"Supplicate to God during times of joy, so that He may answer during times of hardship."

Abu Darda

— 9 —

Supplication Is the Heart of Worship[26]

In the land of Iraq, near the city of Mosul, there was once a village called Nineveh (*Ninwa*). The people of the village had deviated far from the straight path and began worshipping idols, associating many partners with God. But God only wanted good for them and wished to guide them to the truth. For this reason, God sent Prophet Jonah (*Yunus*, PBUH) to these people to help guide them in their faith. He wanted to persuade them to abandon their idols, which could neither benefit nor harm them, in order to worship God alone.

The people of Nineveh rejected Prophet Jonah's (PBUH)

---

[26] Summary of the story of Prophet Yunus (PBUH), Qisas Al-Anbiyaa', pg. 170-176, by Imam Ismail Ibn Kathir.

message to have faith in God and stubbornly continued to worship their idols, misguided by their disbelief. They were hostile toward him and even denied that he was a prophet. They went so far as to call Prophet Jonah (PBUH) a liar, and they rebelliously mocked and ridiculed him.

Not a single person from the people of Nineveh believed in God. Prophet Jonah (PBUH) became upset and felt helpless about his people. The mission seemed futile for Jonah (PBUH); he felt that the people would never believe him or in his message. Only then did God reveal to Jonah (PBUH) that he should warn his people that God was going to punish them because of their continued disbelief. Prophet Jonah did as he was ordered. He warned his people that God's punishment and torment upon them were imminent, and that it was their very last chance to believe. He then did something that God did not order him to do: Prophet Jonah left the village, abandoning his people.

Once his people found out that he had left the village, they realized that the punishment was in fact going to soon reign down upon them. Jonah (PBUH) was not lying and he must truly be a prophet of God, the people recognized. They swiftly repented to God, regretting what they had done to their prophet. Everyone in the village, even the animals and the children, went outside in crowds to make supplication to God. Wailing and crying, they asked God to forgive them and accept their repentance. God, out of His infinite knowledge and mercy, knew the sincerity of their repentance and true faith. He accepted their repentance and lifted the punishment from the people of Nineveh.

Meanwhile, Prophet Jonah (PBUH) had gone to the seashore. He boarded a ship, and set sail. But when the ship reached the middle of the sea, far from any land, a big wave erupted and began tossing the ship. Strong winds tilted the boat that was beginning to overturn. The people on board the ship, fearing that the ship might capsize or sink, started throwing the heaviest cargo overboard to lighten the load and steady the ship, but still the ship would not balance. The turbulence continued, rocking the boat. The ship tilted right and left.

The sailors tried everything they could, and God mentioned them in the Quran:

"*It is He who enables you to travel on land and sea until when you are in ships and they sail with them by a good wind and they rejoice therein, there comes a storm wind and the waves come upon them from everywhere and they assume that they are surrounded, supplicating God, sincere to Him in religion, 'If You should save us from this, we will surely be among the thankful.'*"[27]

The people on the ship concluded that they needed a strategy, and agreed that someone on board would have to jump off of the ship in order to save the rest. They decided to draw a lottery; whoever was selected would have to jump overboard. The lottery settled on Prophet Jonah (PBUH) but the people on the ship refused to allow him to be thrown. They repeated the lottery twice more, but every time it was Prophet Jonah's (PBUH) name that was picked. After the third time, Prophet Jonah (PBUH) knew that he was destined to be chosen. He jumped off of the ship, thereby saving the lives of the remaining people onboard.

Prophet Jonah (PBUH) was not alone in the sea, for a large whale awaited him. God ordered the whale to swallow Jonah (PBUH) in one piece, without piercing his flesh or breaking his bones. God mentions in the Quran, "*And indeed, Jonah was among the messengers. (Mention) when*

---

[27] [Yunus:22]

he ran away to the laden ship. And he drew lots and was among the losers. Then the fish swallowed him, while he was blameworthy."[28] Jonah (PBUH) remained in the stomach of the whale for some time, all the while praising God, making supplication, and asking the Almighty to save him from this astonishing calamity. While inside the whale, Jonah (PBUH) realized his mistake of leaving his people before God had ordered him to do so. He repented sincerely to God, and he made his heartfelt supplication: "*There is no deity except You; exalted are You. Indeed, I have been of the wrongdoers.*"[29]

When the time was right, God made the whale hurl Jonah (PBUH) out on the shore, and made a big vine with wide leaves grow next to him to protect him, cover him, and shade him from the hot sun. As mentioned in the Quran, "*We threw him onto the open shore while he was ill. And We caused to grow over him a gourd vine.*"[30] God ordered Jonah to go back to his people to tell them that He had accepted their repentance and had forgiven them. Jonah (PBUH) obeyed God's orders and did exactly that. Ecstatic to see him return, his people wholeheartedly believed in him and accepted him as their prophet. To reward them, God blessed them in their wealth and their children. God mentioned, "*We sent him to (his people of) a hundred thousand or more. And they believed, so We gave them enjoyment (of life) for a time.*"[31]

Prophet Muhammad (PBUH) has told us that whoever experiences a calamity or endures misfortune then makes the supplication of Prophet Jonah (PBUH), God will relieve him of his calamity. Furthermore, Prophet Muhammad (PBUH) once said that if any Muslim makes the same supplication that Prophet Jonah (PBUH) made inside the stomach of the

---

[28] [Al-Saffaat:139-142]
[29] [Al-Anbiya:87]
[30] [Al-Saffaat:145-146]
[31] [Al-Saffaat:147-148]

whale, God will surely respond and accept it.[32]

---

[32] Narrated by al-Tirmidhi.

Lessons Learned:

1. **Patiently Avoiding Despair when Calling Others to God**
   Jonah (PBUH) was patient for a long time with his people's stubbornness, ridicule, and mockery of him and his message, but in the end he grew upset, despairing that they would never accept his call to God. Once he threatened them with God's punishment followed by his abandonment of them, they repented with sincerity and became believers. There is no place for despair when it comes to repairing the hearts and calling others to God, ever.

2. **Calling to God's Path Will Never Be Easy or Simple**
   Attempting to remove the residue of falsehood and misguidance, as well as the habits, rituals, and traditions that are entrenched in the heart will inevitably be challenging, and will never be easy.

3. **Anger Leads to Devastating Consequences**
   Never make any decisions while in a state of anger. Regret will only follow, just as Prophet Jonah (PBUH) regretted abandoning his people prematurely out of frustration. Prophet Jonah realized that he had incurred upon himself the punishment of God, being swallowed by a whale, because he had made a rash decision when he was upset.

4. **Collective Repentance and Prayer Is Protection from God's Punishment**
   God teaches us that the repentance from sin, even if its punishment has been promised, may still be accepted through collective repentance, humility, supplication, and tears. Although everyone prays individually with one's own words, God, the All-Merciful, looks upon a group together and forgives

them collectively. This is what God did for the community of Jonah (PBUH).

5. **Remember God During Prosperity; He Will Remember You in Adversity**
Because Prophet Jonah (PBUH) always remembered God during his better times and repented to Him, God remembered him in his time of distress by ordering the whale to hurl him onto the shore. Thus, he was able to return to his people and to call over one-hundred-thousand people to become believers in God.

6. **Repentance and Admission of Guilt When Having Wronged Oneself**
Prophet Jonah (PBUH) knew that God had tested him only because He loved him. He also knew that tribulations only increase a person's rank and status and bring about the forgiveness of sins. Therefore, he accepted his trial and admitted that he had only wronged himself. He repented and turned to God whole-heartedly, so God forgave him and ultimately gave him victory.

7. **Supplication Is the Essence of Worship**
Out of God's mercy to Prophet Jonah (PBUH), God answered his prayer, bringing good news to the believers. As God says in the Quran, "*So We responded to him and saved him from distress. And thus do We save the believers.*"[33] Do not be shy to petition God and supplicate often. One never knows how much goodness will come as a result of one's supplication.

---

[33] [Al-Anbiya:88]

"Remove numerous hardships with supplication (duaa)."

Ali Ibn Abi Talib

— 10 —

Supplication: Relief from Distress
The Story of Al-Hajjaj and Hasan Al-Basri [34]

Al-Hajjaj Ibn Yusuf was a tyrannical ruler who governed the state of Iraq during part of the first Hijri century. His power and oppression increased day by day. Dismayed by Al-Hajjaj's difficult rule, many scholars of the time tried to object to his ways. Hasan Al-Basri was one of those scholars, compelled to stand up to this tyrant and decry his bad deeds.

Al-Hajjaj had just built a beautiful mansion for himself in the city of Wasit between the cities of Basra and Kufa in Iraq. The mansion was one of grandeur and splendor, and Al-Hajjaj flaunted the stately abode. He wanted to boast about his wealth, possessions, and power before his own people,

---

[34] Summary of the story of Prophet Yunus (PBUH), Qisas Al-Anbiyaa', pg. 170-176, by Imam Ismail Ibn Kathir.

as many tyrants do. Hasan Al-Basri, however, who was from the nearby city of Basra, was not impressed by Al-Hajjaj's exorbitantly excessive dwelling. Instead, he took Al-Hajjaj's boastful demeanor as an opportunity to advise, remind, and divert the attention of those naive enough to gather around his bogus, worldly distractions. He wanted to direct people to the brilliance of God's absolute and infinite perfection.

Hasan Al-Basri set out to the mansion and he was determined to address the residents of the city who were enamored by the grand structure. At last, Hasan Al-Basri reached the crowd standing in awe of the exquisitely built architectural masterpiece. He advised the crowd not to overrate the frivolous joys of life and forget what would ultimately be the greater prize. He stood before them and announced:

"We have witnessed what this insidious man has constructed, but we find that Pharoah had once built more colossal monuments than what has been built here and more towering structures than this. Yet God destroyed Pharaoh and all that he ever built from fame to fortune ... If only Al-Hajjaj knew that the Heavens are revolted by him and that his people have deluded him!"

Hasan Al-Basri continued to implore the people, trying his best to expose Al-Hajjaj's pettiness until even the audience pitied him. One listener responded compassionately, "That is enough, father of Saeed. What you have said will suffice." To this, Hasan swiftly replied, "The scholars are accountable to God to teach and advise the people, and to not withhold any information that may be of benefit to them!"

Al-Hajjaj heard about the commotion that was being made and what was said of him, and his heart filled with rage. He called a meeting with his councilmen the very next day, and he said to them furiously, "Curse you all! May you all be destroyed! I cannot believe that a servant from Basra has the nerve to speak of us like this as he pleases, and that he is not challenged by anyone from amongst you to debate or silence him! I swear that I will get him myself and have you all drink from his blood, you group of cowards!"

Al-Hajjaj ordered his chief interrogator and his executioner to his throne immediately. He commanded the guards to bring Hasan Al-Basri swiftly. There was a gloomy atmosphere pervading the court, for they all feared for Hasan Al-Basri and what was to come.

Alas, Hasan Al-Basri was now in the presence of Al-Hajjaj. He looked around the court, knowing his near future appeared bleak, and he muttered something quietly under his breath. Then, Hasan proudly advanced toward Al-Hajjaj, walking poised with his head held high. With an air of certainty in God, the Almighty, in fear of nothing but Him, he possessed the confidence that only a believer possesses.

Al-Hajjaj was taken aback, for he did not expect such assertion from Hasan Al-Basri. Bewildered yet amazed, he said, "Come closer, father of Saeed, come closer!" Al-Hajjaj called him forward again and again until Hasan Al-Basri was so close that he was sitting on the same royal cushion as Al-Hajjaj. The people in the court watched very closely in astonishment. What was happening?

Al-Hajjaj then asked Hasan Al-Basri about some religious matters, and Hasan Al-Basri did not cease to impress him with the answers that came from his wealth of knowledge, logic, and confidence. Al-Hajjaj then declared, "You are truly an exceptional scholar, father of Saeed!" As a token of his admiration, before they parted Al-Hajjaj presented some of his most expensive perfume for Hasan Al-Basri to apply, an

Arab tradition.

As he was leaving the court, Al-Hajjaj's assistant followed Hasan Al-Basri out and then asked, "Al-Hajjaj ordered you here with a vile plan that he did not fulfill. I saw you muttering something quietly under your breath after you saw what was in store for you. So what did you say?"

Hasan Al-Basri replied, "Oh God, my Sustainer, my Safe-Haven. Make his revenge as peaceful and cool for me as You made the fire for our prophet Abraham."

Lessons Learned:

1. **All Tyrants Have the Same Approach**
    We notice that all oppressors, no matter what their
    time or place in history, have similar habits of
    building monuments, architectural masterpieces, and
    other worldly attractions as a way to exhibit their
    pride, self-conceit, and superiority over their people.
    Furthermore, should anyone among their people ever
    disagree with them, they are willing to take every
    measure to stop the dissenters, even if it results in
    torture or murder.

2. **Wisdom in Selecting the Time to Enjoin the Right
    and Forbid the Wrong**
    We notice from the story that Hasan Al-Basri chose
    the ideal time to advise people, while they were
    gathered in admiration of the pretentious structure.
    He wanted to teach them that no matter how much
    wealth they acquired, how large their houses were,
    or how great their worldly possessions might be, all
    these trivial things would vanish. Only their deeds
    would remain. He persuaded them by illustrating
    the story of Pharaoh, and how worldly belongings
    did not ultimately benefit him. Additionally, Hasan
    Al-Basri tried to advise and guide Al-Hajjaj as well.
    Those around Al-Hajjaj had fueled the delusion that
    caused him to err. Hasan Al-Basri further told him
    that the angels in heaven despised him because of
    his injustice to those who were under his authority.
    Therefore, Hasan Al-Basri did not only advise the
    people, but also their leader.

3. **Guiding People Using Stories and Examples**
    Notice that Hasan Al-Basri did not preach to people
    by using scripture and teachings of the Prophet

(PBUH) alone, but also utilized examples and stories. Using such techniques to advise tends to be more convincing, and encourages the listener to ponder and understand. Such was the teaching of our beloved Prophet Muhammad (PBUH).

4. **Whoever Truly Fears God, God Provides for Them a Way Out**[35]
Hasan Al-Basri did not fear the ruler even though he knew that Al-Hajjaj was planning to kill him. Hasan Al-Basri knew that God would surely provide a way out for him. His trust and absolute confidence in God, along with his pure intention in advising the people, seeking the pleasure of God alone, gave him this strength.

5. **Remaining Steadfast Will Increase One in Prestige and Respect**
When Hasan Al-Basri entered Al-Hajjaj's palace, he was strong and confident. He had complete belief that his fate was in God's hands. Because he did not enter with trepidation or humiliation, Al-Hajjaj was compelled not only to fear him, but to also respect him.

6. **The Importance of Supplication (*Duaa*)**
Supplication is a form or worship. Whenever the believers are in crisis, they must turn to face God and fall back upon Him. In this story, when Hasan Al-Basri needed God's help, his supplication was not one of the dictum supplications, but rather one that came from the heart and mind. These words saved him from the tyranny of Al-Hajjaj, and they changed his fate from being murdered to one who was ultimately revered. As a result, Al-Hajjaj appointed Hasan Al-Basri as a distinguished member of his closest circle.

---

[35] [Al-Tawba:2]

Therefore, simply using one's own words to ask God for anything at any time brings about solutions in even the most trying circumstances. God does not look at one's words, but rather at one's heart and mind.

"*Seize the opportunity of supplication (duaa); for whoever knocks on the door numerous times will find that it will open for him.*"

Abu Darda
Narrated by Al-Hassan

— 11 —
The Acceptance of True Supplication
The Story of Moses (PBUH) and the Wrongdoer[36]

Supplication is very powerful when it is done right. Let us travel together to Prophet Moses' time (PBUH) to see how powerful true supplication can be ...

A severe drought fell upon the Children of Israel (*Bani Israil*) during the time of Prophet Moses (PBUH). All of the villagers gathered together and stormed over to Prophet Moses (PBUH). "Oh Speaker to God, pray to God to send showers upon us and end this drought!" they cried out for help. So Prophet Moses (PBUH) stood up and joined the crowd in the middle of the desert. There were more than seventy-thousand people in standing, raising their hands to God, waiting for Prophet Moses (PBUH) to begin his

---

[36] Al-Tawwabeen, Author Ibn Qudamah.

supplication.

Prophet Moses (PBUH) began, "Oh God, pour down rain upon us to end this drought, and spread upon us Your mercy. Oh God, bestow Your mercy on the nursing babies, the drinking animals, and the elderly who kneel in prayer toward You."

Then, to the astonishment of Prophet Moses (PBUH) and all those watching, the few scattered clouds that were in the sky vanished, heat poured down, and the drought intensified.

"What is happening?" those in the crowd exclaimed. Prophet Moses (PBUH) was surprised as well. He asked God about what had transpired. It was revealed to Prophet Moses (PBUH) that there was a sinner in the gathering who had been prominent in disobeying God for forty years. Prophet Moses should call upon his people to ask this man to leave the congregation.

Prophet Moses (PBUH) pleaded to God, "Dear God, I am only one frail servant. My voice is weak; how will it reach them when there are more than seventy-thousand people?" Then God revealed to Moses (PBUH) that he should do his part, and then leave the rest to Him. Prophet Moses (PBUH) raised his voice with all his might, "Oh defiant servant, you have opposed God for forty years with your disobedience! Come out from amongst us! Due to your sin, we have been deprived of rain!" cried Moses (PBUH).

The guilty man waited, looking left and right, hoping that someone else would step forward. No one did. He sunk his head down into his garment with deep regret, knowing that he was surely the one, and felt guilty of his sins. The man was conflicted as to what he should do, but he realized that

73

if he stayed amongst the congregation, all would continue to suffer because of him. However, if he stepped forward, he would be humiliated forever in his community. The man remorsefully raised his hands with a sincerity that he had never before known, and with a humility that he had never previously exhibited. As tears poured down both cheeks, he said with true sincerity, he said, "My Lord, my Master, I disobeyed you for forty years, yet you provided for me; now I come to you in true obedience, so please accept it from me!"

Prophet Moses (PBUH) and the Children of Israel waited for the sinner to step forward, yet no one did. No sooner had the man finished his supplication than did a heavy cloud appeared in the sky, and rain began to pour. Prophet Moses (PBUH) called out, "My Lord and Master, for what reason have you blessed us with rain when no one has come forward from amongst us?"

God revealed to Moses (PBUH), "Oh Moses, you were given rain because of the same person who caused you to be deprived from it."

Prophet Moses (PBUH) wanted to know who the repentant man was who had earned God's forgiveness. He asked, "Show me your obedient servant!"

God revealed to Moses (PBUH), "Oh Moses, if I did not expose him when he defied Me, would I disclose his identity once he obeys Me?"

Lessons Learned:

1. **Supplication Is Not Only for the Prophets and the Very Religious**
   Many believe that God only accepts and answers the prayers of the Prophets and those who are extremely religious because they are the ones who draw closest to God, by remembering God often and performing continuous acts of devotion. But if we turn to our Lord with sincere intentions, we will find Him with us, and we will not be left disappointed. God is merciful, and He is indeed waiting for our repentance. The sinner in the story above disobeyed God for forty years, yet God did not hesitate to accept his repentance. Let us not underestimate the greatness and power of true supplication. As Ibn Qayyim said, "*If the heart is true and is joined with pure intentions and sincerity, then our supplication will be accepted.*"

2. **Mentioning the Good in Supplication (*Duaa*)**
   As we noticed, Prophet Moses (PBUH) pleaded to God for the nursing babies who were too young to sin, for the poor animals who needed water to stay alive, and for the elderly who had vowed to draw as close as possible to God for the remainder of their lives. Moses (PBUH) mentioned deserving members of the society who needed water to survive and who embodied goodness. We should also do good (pray on time, fast, give charity, exhibit patience with people, and help a friend in need among many other things), so we can plead by these actions when we supplicate to God.

3. **Bad Deeds Prevent Supplication (*Duaa*) from Being Accepted**

   We often pray and make supplication, yet many of our prayers are not answered. We begin to question why our supplication (*duaa*) is not accepted. We should review our lives and our actions and think seriously about our failings, whether small or large. We should try to correct ourselves. Our behavior can harm an entire community, not just ourselves. The sinner in the story did not even think the call was for him because he thought his transgressions were very slight. He did not realize that his sins were indeed significant enough to warrant God's wrath. We must, therefore take ourselves into account for our own sins before we are questioned about them before God.

4. **The Destruction of an Entire Nation Can Be Due to the Sins of Just One**

   Many of us are convinced that we, as individuals, are responsible for our own sins, and that we alone will be punished for them. But the truth is that perhaps our wrongdoings are the cause of a calamity that affects many others, such as loss of employment, or victory being withheld during a nation's fight for freedom. Our sole acts of disobedience may even warrant God's wrath in the form of a drought, earthquake, or flood, among other disasters. Distance yourself from God's fury and protect yourself through good actions, thereby protecting those around you. We should never underestimate the power of our own sins. Let us work together to minimize the occurrence of our bad deeds, and make sincere repentance for our past transgressions.

5. **Humility, Supplication, and Repentance Lead to God's Acceptance**

   We noticed that the sinner broke down in front of God; he offered his most sincere repentance in order to show God his sincerity. He begged that he would not be exposed in front of his entire community. God accepted his repentance and accepted his prayer. Imagine that because of this same person, a whole community had suffered, yet in a matter of one truthful minute of supplication and sincere repentance to God, all was forgiven and the community's ability to survive was restored. This is the power of true and sincere repentance.

6. **God Is the Concealer (*Al-Sattar*)**

   God conceals sins and forgives them for us, yet we often expose each other's faults and actions, without thinking. God refused to even expose this man to His prophet. God's explanation is clear: if He did not expose him while he sinned, why then expose him once he repented? This also gives us the insight that discretion in regard to someone else's wrong deeds should be upheld, because we never know when a person might repent. Our words may also be counted against us as bad deeds. We should conceal the mistakes of others so that God may conceal our own.

7. **The Importance of Supplication and Showing Gratitude for Blessings**

   God has showered many of us with blessings, including good health, safety, children, and even rain. However, we forget to thank Him for all of these abundant blessings as if God is required to give them to us, as though we are entitled to them. We forget that all of our blessings could vanish in the blink of an eye. Let us be vigilant and remember to thank God for the copious blessings He has bestowed upon us. We must search for ways to thank God so that He will continue to bless us and provide for us.

8. **Supplication (*Duaa*) in Congregation Brings About Its Acceptance**

The Children of Israel (*Bani Israil*) had many issues and problems among themselves, but when drought occurred they united together as one. They collectively asked God for His mercy and blessings. We, too, should overlook our differences and our petty issues with one another, be them with an acquaintance at the Mosque, a colleague at work or in school, or even a relative whether close or distant. We must strive to become one strong, united community, capable of overcoming the obstacles that hinder our success. That way, God will send down His mercy upon us, and accept and answer our supplications, God willing.

"Oh you who believe, eat from the good things which We have provided for you and be grateful to God if it is (indeed sincerely) Him that you worship."

[Al-Baqarah:172]

— 12 —

The Etiquette of Eating

The Story of Um Ma'bed During the Prophet
Muhammad's (PBUH) Migration [37]

It was narrated by Abu Ma'bed that during the migration of Prophet Muhammad (PBUH) from Mecca to Madinah, the Prophet passed by the tent of Um Ma'bed to rest and to seek out provision of either food or drink.

The Prophet (PBUH) greeted Um Ma'bed and asked her if she had meat or dates he could buy, but she replied that she had no food to sell. He noticed that she did have a sheep, though it looked frail and scrawny. Nevertheless, he inquired about the sheep. She replied that the sheep was of no use; it was so weak and tired that it fell behind the rest of the sheep. The Prophet (PBUH) asked if the sheep might still have any

---

[37] Al-Rahiq Al-Makhtum, pg. 153-154, by Safi-ur-Rahman Al-Mubarkpuri, and from Tabaqaat Ibn Saad.

milk for them to drink. Um Ma'bed replied that surely there was no hope that the sheep could produce any milk, since the sheep was much too feeble.

The Prophet (PBUH) asked Um Ma'bed's permission to try to milk the sheep anyway. She freely granted him permission. The Prophet (PBUH) massaged the sheep and mentioned God's name, and said: "Oh God, bless her sheep."

The Prophet (PBUH) asked for a container. Miraculously, the sheep produced milk, and he was able to fill the container until it was full. The Prophet (PBUH) gave Um Ma'bed the container to drink first, and she continued to drink until she was completely full. He then gave the container to his companions, who likewise drank until they too were entirely satiated. Finally, the Prophet (PBUH) drank from the container himself until he was also full. He mentioned that the one who brings forth the drink should be last to drink, referring to himself.

The Prophet (PBUH) milked the sheep one final time, leaving the container completely full for Um Ma'bed to keep for her household. The Prophet (PBUH) and his companions then departed.

Later that day, Abu Ma'bed returned, and was surprised to find the container full of milk. Puzzled, he wondered where the milk could have come from, since their sheep was too frail to give milk. Upon asking his wife about it, Um Ma'bed told him that a blessed man had passed by, and she continued to describe the Prophet's (PBUH) actions and words. Abu Ma'bed was intrigued and impressed. He ascertained that the Prophet must be a person from the tribe of Quraish, and he vowed that, if he had met him, he would have followed him on the straight path. He swore he would do so if he could find a way.

Lessons Learned:

1. **Treating Others Kindly Opens the Hearts**
   The Prophet (PBUH) treated Um Ma'bed with kindness by greeting her graciously. He offered to purchase provisions from her instead of asking her to give him food. Additionally, he (PBUH) then asked her permission to milk the sheep, gave her the first drink, and asked her to continue drinking until she was satiated. He also left a full container for her family before leaving. This gentle approach displaying impeccable manners made Um Ma'bed reciprocate kindness and trust him. Likewise, his kind treatment made her speak positively about him when she described him to her husband. Her husband's heart also became inclined toward the Prophet (PBUH) without ever having met him.

2. **Conditions to Have Blessings in One's Food**
   The Prophet (PBUH) taught us the conditions for our food to be blessed. Among them is to have complete trust in God, that He is the Provider. Another is to say "*Bismillah*" thereby mentioning God's name before starting a meal, and to make supplications before and upon commencing, asking God to bless the food. By doing so, not only will the food and drink be blessed, but the one consuming them will be blessed as well.

3. **The Leader Is Last to Eat or Drink**
   The Prophet (PBUH) was the last to drink from the milk. Leaders should ensure that those under their supervision are well taken care of, which means that their followers come first, even before the leaders themselves. This should be applied and practiced in a variety of situations. Unfortunately, one can witness

today how present-day leaders do the opposite of this prophetic teaching, consuming only the best for themselves and leaving their people hungry and needy.

4. **Eating and Drinking Only One's Fill, Being Considerate of Those Who Have Not Yet Eaten**
The Prophet (PBUH) was a guest when passing through the tent of Um Ma'bed. He was in need of food and rest, and Um Ma'bed was gracious enough to provide him with what little she could. As a guest, the Prophet (PBUH) remembered to leave the container full when he left, thoughtfully keeping in mind members of Um Ma'bed's family who may return hungry. When given food as a guest or when eating in a group, visitors should feel free to eat or drink as much as they need. However, they should also remember to be considerate and leave some for those around them, including the host and his or her family.

5. **Islam Can Spread Through Good Character**
The way Um Ma'bed described the Prophet's (PBUH) impressive character led Abu Ma'bed to yearn to be the Prophet's friend and follower. Practicing good character is the only right way to deal with others. God rewards such behavior in the hereafter, as well as earning one respect in this lifetime. Good character spreads the faith in the best of ways without preaching a word.

6. **Miracle of the Prophet (PBUH)**
It was a miracle and a blessing for the Prophet (PBUH) to be able to milk the frail, weak sheep. Although miracles may be beyond our grasp, God provides blessings in our families, actions, wealth, and in the value of our time. God gives benefit beyond what could ever be expected to those who

trust in Him and follow His straight path with sincerity and good intentions.

Luqman told his son, "Oh son, if the stomach gets too full, ideas will sleep, wisdom will be muted, and the limbs will sit without worship."

— 13 —

The Food of the Generous Is Medicine
The Story of Imam Ahmad Hosting Imam Al-Shafi [38]

Long ago, Imam Ahmad Ibn Hanbal used to extol Imam Al-Shafi's knowledge and piety, often mentioning him to his daughter. One day, Imam Ahmad invited Imam Al-Shafi to his house for an extended visit. After enjoying dinner together, Imam Al-Shafi retired for the evening and headed off to bed.

The next morning, Imam Ahmad's daughter had a peculiar question: Why did he always praise Imam Al-Shafi for his virtues and his piety? The young girl had not seen him pray, read the Quran, or praise God the previous night, she explained to her father. In addition she had noticed three

[38] Narrated by Dr. Urayfi, mention in Min Rawai' Al-Qisas, from Zaad Al-Murabieen by Shaikh Nabil Al-Awadi.

strange things.

When her father asked her about her observations, Imam Ahmad's daughter replied, "First, when we offered him food to eat, he did not eat a modest amount in the manner in which the pious should eat. Second, when he went to sleep, he did not pray the extra nightly prayers. Finally, when he prayed the morning prayer (*fajr*) with us, he did not make ablution (*wudu*)."

When Imam Al-Shafi woke up, Imam Ahmad mentioned to him what his daughter had noticed. Imam Al-Shafi replied, "Oh father of Muhammad, I ate a large amount because I know your food is lawful (*halal*), and I know you are a generous person. The food of a generous person is known to be like medicine while the food of a miser is like a disease. I was not eating to get full, but rather to be healed of ailments. Also, I did not sleep during the night because when I laid myself down, God opened my eyes to seventy-two issues of jurisprudence (*fiqh*) for the benefit of the Muslims, so that is what prevented me from sleeping. Finally, I did not make ablution (*wudu*) for the morning prayer (*fajr*) because I did not sleep at all, so I did not nullify my ablution (*wudu*) from the evening prayer (*isha*)."

When Imam Al-Shafi left, Imam Ahmad turned to his daughter and told her that what Imam Al-Shafi did while resting was more virtuous than what he did himself while standing up all night in prayer.

Lessons Learned:

1. **Fathers Are Role Models**
   Imam Ahmad was a shining example of a father acting as a role model for his daughter. He used to share his knowledge at home, and teach his children about his teachers and their knowledge. Therefore, his children were inquisitive and eager to learn more. Today, many parents attend lectures and classes, but they fail to convey what they have learned to their wives and children. As a result, one will find a father who is pious, faithful, and knowledgeable, yet the knowledge possessed by his family is negligible, leaving their actions to reflect their limited understanding. This problem stems from parents failing to assume full responsibility for their children. They forget the words of our beloved Prophet Muhammad (PBUH), who once said, *"You are a shepherd, and each of you is responsible for his flock."*[39]

2. **A Variety of Deeds Can Cultivate Piety**
   We note that the daughter of Imam Ahmad measured the degree of piety of Imam Al-Shafi by how long he prayed at night, praised God, and recited from the Quran. These acts of worship purify the heart and raise the status of the believer in this life and in the hereafter. This is why Imam Ahmad's daughter questioned how Imam Al-Shafi could be so devout if he did not perform these acts of worships. She learned that piety can be fostered from a variety of deeds; it is not restricted to just these limited acts of devotion.

---

[39] Narrated by Imam Ahmed.

3. **The Food of the Generous Is Like Medicine**
   God blesses the food of a generous person who loves
   to graciously host his guests. Therefore, his food
   becomes like a cure to their sicknesses and ailments.
   We should never be miserly with guests, because
   they are indeed God's guests, and God is the most
   generous of hosts. Our food should be like medicine
   for them rather than an affliction upon them.

4. **With Lawful (*Halal*) Food Comes God's Blessings**
   God is pure, and he only accepts what is pure. In the
   Quran, God says, "*O Mankind, eat from whatever
   is on earth that is lawful and pure, and do not follow
   the footsteps of Satan. Indeed he is to you a clear
   enemy.*"[40] The believing women used to tell their
   husbands that they could tolerate hunger, but they
   could not tolerate the unlawful (*haram*). Therefore,
   we should be among those who always make sure
   our food is lawful (*halal*), so that God will accept our
   supplications (*duaa*), bless our households, heal us,
   and provide for us in ways we never expect.

5. **Seeking Knowledge Is Greater Than Night Prayer**
   We note that Imam Al-Shafi realized that pursuing
   religious knowledge in order to teach is yet another
   act of worship, and the reward for it is better than
   that of praying all night. Prophet Muhammad
   (PBUH) said: "*An hour of reflection is better than a
   night full of prayer.*"[41] Therefore, we should purify
   our intentions and get closer to God by learning
   beneficial knowledge. We should use what we
   learn to simultaneously be of service to the greater
   community.

---

[40] [Al-Baqarah:168]
[41] Sound narration (*gharib*).

6. There is No Shyness When Asking About Matters of Religion

Imam Ahmad's daughter was not shy when asking her father about the actions of Imam Al-Shafi. Instead of drawing her own conclusions from her assumptions, she asked her father who, likewise, avoided his own interpretation of Imam Al-Shafi's actions. Rather, Imam Ahmad posed her questions directly to him to hear his explanation. Furthermore, Imam Al-Shafi was not upset by the questioning of his actions; he was understanding, and kindly answered all of them willingly. This reminds us that we should accept criticism and answer questions tenderly, without becoming overly sensitive, combative, or easily upset.

7. Have the Best Opinion of People

It is only human nature to draw assumptions from various scenarios and to jump to conclusions. However, it is imperative for every Muslim to give others the benefit of the doubt, and to always have the best opinion of other people. The Prophet (PBUH) said, "*If one of your friends errs, make seventy excuses for him. If your hearts are unable to do so, then know that the shortcoming is in your own selves.*" Giving seventy excuses humbles the heart and reminds us to be forgiving. It also causes us to recognize that only God sees and knows all things, especially the secrets of the heart.

"*If a person seeks knowledge, but neglects the actions to implement it, and if a person speaks of his love of others with his tongue yet breaks ties of kinship, God will curse him, make him mute, and cause him to go blind.*"

Hasan Al-Basri

— 14 —
Charity Begins at Home
The Story of Abu Bakr and Mistah [42]

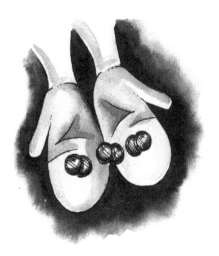

Abu Bakr Al-Siddiq, may God be pleased with him, was very generous with his wealth. He would often give much in charity to the poor and the needy. Among those upon whom he would spend, Abu Bakr used to provide for his nephew, Mistah bin Uthathah, who was very poor. Abu Bakr was generous to his nephew and provided for Mistah throughout his life, starting from the early age of four years old.

As Mistah grew, so did his devotion to the cause of Islam. Mistah was one of the companions of the Prophet (PBUH) who nobly engaged in the battle of Badr. Abu Bakr continued over the years to provide for Mistah in kindness.

---

[42] Tafsir al-Qurtubi, Volume 6, pg 4742.

Years after the battle, a difficult tribulation befell the Prophet's (PBUH) household. Rumors and suspicion had spread, and Aisha, the wife of the Prophet (PBUH) and daughter of Abu Bakr Al-Siddiq, was accused of adultery. Reclaiming her innocence from the false slander, Aisha rejoiced when God revealed the following verse in the Quran:

"Indeed, those who came with falsehood are a group among you. Do not think it bad for you; rather it is good for you. For every person among them is what (punishment) he has earned from the sin, and he who took upon himself the greater portion thereof - for him is a great punishment."[43]

The relief was tremendous for her family, but the painful incident was hard to forget, and it was very difficult to forgive those who spread the slander. Abu Bakr knew that even his own nephew Mistah was among the people who had defamed Aisha, so Abu Bakr was both hurt and upset. With the troubling event so fresh in his mind and heart, Abu Bakr declared that he would never spend upon Mistah again. The following verse was then revealed:

"And let not those of virtue among you and wealth swear not to give (aid) to their relatives and the needy and the emigrants for the cause of God, and let them pardon and overlook. Would you not like that God should forgive you? And God is Forgiving and Merciful."[44]

Abu Bakr, may God be pleased with him, despite his anguish and hurt feelings, immediately responded by exclaiming, "By God, I would love it that God forgives me!" Without hesitation, Abu Bakr promptly returned to his long-established habit of giving charity to his nephew, and he swore that he would never again cease spending upon Mistah.

---

[43] [Al-Nur:11]
[44] [Al-Nur:22]

Lessons Learned:

1. **Charity Begins at Home**

   The story of Abu Bakr and his nephew Mistah
   teaches us a great lesson. Relatives take priority over
   others and are the most deserving when it comes
   to receiving charity. God mentions the virtue of
   taking care of relatives immediately after mentioning
   parents, as stated in the following verse from the
   Quran: *"They ask you, (O Muhammad), what they
   should spend. Say, 'Whatever you spend of good is
   (to be) for parents and relatives and orphans and the
   needy and the traveler.'"*[45] And Prophet Muhammad
   (PBUH) said: *"Charity to the needy is rewarded, but
   charity to family members is double the reward. One
   reward is for the charity and one reward is for taking
   care of family."*[46] Do not be among those who miss
   out on the tremendous reward given to those who
   keep ties of kinship by forgetting relatives such as
   uncles and aunts. A person can take advantage of
   fulfilling such acts of devotion simply by asking
   about family members or giving gifts or charity.
   By keeping ties of kinship strong, we maintain our
   closeness with God.

2. **Trials Test the Weak**

   Mistah was one of the companions who witnessed
   the battle of Badr and the Prophet (PBUH) said:
   *"Perhaps God looked upon the Badr warriors and said,
   'Do whatever you like, for I have ordained that you
   will be in Paradise, or I forgave you.'"*[47] Still, Mistah
   did indeed take part in the spread of rumors that he

---

[45] [Al-Baqarah:215]

[46] Narrated by Al-Tirmidhi.

[47] Narrated by Al-Bukhari and Muslim.

94

had heard without verifying their veracity. However, when God revealed the innocence of Aisha, Mistah repented and asked God for forgiveness. This shows that no matter how strong of faith we might be, it is still possible that we may waiver when we face trials and tests of faith. Therefore, we should ask God to help prevent us from falling into error, and if we do, it is upon us to ask God for forgiveness.

3. **Refraining from Retribution Brings Great Reward**
Abu Bakr did not make the intention to cut off Mistah before the verse declared his daughter's innocence. Abu Bakr was well aware that Mistah was one of the people who had spoken ill about Aisha, but he did not stop spending on him, so God rewarded him by proving the innocence of his daughter and honoring him with a verse that was revealed specifically for her. A believer should not deal with others based on their reciprocal treatment, but rather treat others in a way that is most pleasing to God.

4. **React Positively, Even When Wronged**
God reminded Abu Bakr to react positively in two ways. First, God reminded Abu Bakr that Mistah was one of his relatives, was needy, and was from those who relocated for the sake of God. Abu Bakr should therefore be compassionate toward him. Moreover, God reminded Abu Bakr that he had the upper hand because he had been favored and he was the one who had wealth, so he should choose to react positively in his judgment of Mistah by continuing his benevolence and refraining from cutting him off. Perhaps God wanted to teach the valuable lesson that we should avoid judging others based on how they have personally wronged us, just as we should avoid forgetting all of the goodness they have done. We

should abstain from allowing personal vengeance to become a punishment for others.

5. **God's Forgiveness Comes by Pardoning Others**
Abu Bakr immediately heeded God's orders, promptly forgave Mistah, and instantly returned to providing for him because Abu Bakr wanted to earn God's forgiveness. We, too, should quickly pardon those who wrong us so we can likewise earn God's forgiveness and great reward.

6. **Charitable Donations Warrant Forgiveness of Sins and Pardoning of Bad Deeds**
God teaches us that charity erases sins and pardons bad deeds. One should strive to be among those who give charity following any bad deed in order to be among those mentioned in the following verse: "… *Would you not like that God should forgive you? And God is Forgiving and Merciful.*"[48]

---

[48] [Al-Nur:22]

Abu Ayyub (may God be pleased with him) reported: A man said to the Prophet (PBUH): "Direct me to a deed which may admit me to Paradise." Upon this he (the Messenger of God (PBUH)) said, "Worship God and never associate anything with Him in worship, establish prayer, pay alms (zakat), and strengthen the ties of kinship."

Prophet Muhammad (PBUH)
Narrated by Al-Bukhari and Muslim

— 15 —
The Fruits of Maintaining Bonds of Kinship [49]

One day, long ago, there was extreme poverty encompassing the Ha'il district in a small town of the Arabian Peninsula in Saudi Arabia. Extreme hunger and starvation overtook them. Despite his poverty, one elderly man decided to set aside his last three coffee beans in case any guests visited him.

One day his sister came to visit him from a nearby village. He was worried that something unpleasant might have happened to her, concerned that there may have been an unfortunate reason for her trip. She smiled and assured him that she had only come to visit because she had missed him and merely wished to see him. She had just wanted to

---

[49] Newspaper article, Ha'il (Riyadh, Saudi Arabia), by Ali Al-Sayir.

have a cup of coffee together.

The man was pleased to have her, and he debated with himself whether he should use the coffee beans he coveted for his guests to make coffee for his sister, or if he should save the coffee beans to host potential future guests. He decided to use the beans to make her a cup of coffee. So he roasted the beans, crushed them, ground them, and brewed them into coffee. He poured a cup for his sister and they had a lovely time together before she left, returning to her village.

The next morning the man heard someone calling him from outside of his house. Startled, he went outside, distraught that it might be a guest from out of town, in which case he would not have anything left to offer the visitor. To his surprise, it was a stranger who came bearing gifts: a camel's load of sugar, coffee, shortening, rice, tea, spices, and fabric. The hefty gift was sent from a merchant he knew who used to live in the same village. The man thanked the courier and asked him to convey his thanks and extend his appreciation to the merchant, promising to visit him soon in order to thank him personally.

As he brought the kind gifts into his home, he exclaimed, "Oh God, I used my last three coffee beans for my sister, so you compensated me with all of this goodness; how generous you are, my Lord!"

Lessons Learned:

1. **Saving Teaches Self-Discipline and Budgeting Skills**
   The man saved his last three coffee beans for potential guests, not to consume them for himself. These days we remember our immediate needs and do not plan for the near future. The Prophet (PBUH) said: *"God will be merciful to the person who earns a living in a good way, spends it in moderation, and saves for his day in need."*[50]

2. **Visiting Others for the Sake of God Is Rewarded**
   The sister visited her brother for the sake of God. Her brother was very pleased to see her and offered her the only remaining morsel he had. The Prophet (PBUH) said, *"Whoever visits a sick person or a brother in faith for the sake of God, God will make the caller (angel) pray that he will be blessed and that his route will be blessed and God will secure a spot for him in Paradise."*[51]

3. **The Blessing of Maintaining Kinship Ties**
   God honored the man and blessed him because of his kindness and because of the way he honored his sister. Prophet Muhammad (PBUH) said, *"Whoever would like God to increase his wealth and bless him with a lengthy life should maintain his ties of kinship."*[52] We should always take care of our parents, grandparents, brothers, sisters, aunts, uncles, and all other remaining relatives, so that we may be rewarded in this life and in the hereafter.

---

[50] Narrated by Al-Hindi, Kanz al-Ummal, Volume 4.
[51] Narrated by Ibn Majah and Tirmidhi.
[52] Narration is agreed upon.

4. **God Is the Best Provider**

   Many of us get busy and preoccupied with thinking about how to make money or earn a living. We forget that, in the end, we receive no more than what God has apportioned for us. When the man in the story offered the only coffee he had to his sister, he did not do so expecting anything in return, or for someone to repay him for his act of goodness to his kin. It is true that we should work hard for our living, but we should also be content with the allotment of our provision. Ali Ibn Abi Talib said, *"Provision is of two kinds: one that you seek, and the other seeks you. The one that seeks you will get to you even if you do not try, and the other that you seek will only get to you if you work hard for it. The first one is a gift, or honor, from God, while the other is out of fairness from God."*

5. **God Is the Most Generous**

   The man was generous and used his last three coffee beans for his sister, but God was yet more generous with him by ultimately providing him with a large quantity of a variety of food. In truth, the scale of God's generosity is incomprehensible in comparison to the generosity of the merchant.